KV-733-742

The Futura Library of Comic Speeches

BUSINESSMEN

6. Comic Speeches for Businessmen

Also from Futura

The Futura Library of Comic Speeches
1. COMIC SPEECHES FOR SPORTSMEN
2. COMIC SPEECHES FOR SOCIAL OCCASIONS
3. COMIC SPEECHES FOR THE LEGAL PROFESSION
4. COMIC SPEECHES FOR THE SALES FORCE
5. COMIC SPEECHES FOR THE MEDICAL PROFESSION

The Futura Library of Comic Speeches

BUSINESSMEN

6. Comic Speeches for Businessmen

Futura

A Futura Book

Copyright © Victorama 1986

First published in Great Britain in 1986
by Futura Publications, A Division of
Macdonald & Co (Publishers) Ltd
London & Sydney

ISBN 0 7088 2990 2

Typeset by Leaper & Gard Ltd., Bristol
Printed and bound in Great Britain by
William Collins, Glasgow

Futura Publications
A Division of
Macdonald & Co (Publishers) Ltd
Greater London House
Hampstead Road
London NW1 7QX
A BPCC plc Company

Contents

PART ONE

*How to make a
public speech*

Introduction

For all but the most extrovert, an invitation to make a public speech is something to be dreaded. But it needn't be, particularly if you are in business or banking — because businessmen and bankers have two significant advantages when it comes to making public speeches. The first is the wide appeal of their subject matter. Think about it for a second. Who doesn't have a funny story to tell about their bank manager? And who hasn't, at some time or other, experienced the unique pleasures and problems of office life? What this means is that when you stand up to give a speech about the worlds of business or banking, you can be confident that most of the people in your audience will be able to identify with you and appreciate your material — and that's an asset that shouldn't be underrated.

The second advantage that can be claimed by businessmen and bankers is their skill at communicating with people. Every businessman worth his salt is versed in the art of persuasion; he knows how to please his clients and customers while getting what he wants. And bankers are used to assessing their customers, weighing up situations and responding appropriately. All these skills are directly applicable when it comes to making a public speech. Like the banker and the businessman, the speaker has to do a lot of preparation; he has to make judgements in advance; he has to decide what he's aiming for and plan his strategy accordingly. And all these skills can be learned.

To help you, this book contains everything needed to turn a businessman or a banker into a public speaker. In it you'll find all the information required to prepare and deliver an amusing speech — from the initial groundwork of assessing your audience, through preparing and delivering your material, to advice on coping with your nerves on the day. And because this is the *complete* guide to comic speechmaking you'll find hundreds of jokes, anecdotes and quotations which will ensure that you're never at a loss for an entertaining word.

Know Your Audience

The only thing you need to do to make your speaking engagement a brilliant success is *please* your audience. It couldn't be much simpler. All you have to do is entertain them with the kind of stories and material they want to hear, and send them away thinking what an amusing person you are. That's the theory, and of course the practice is more difficult. One of the main obstacles to success is fear of failure. Very often speakers just try to ignore the impending ordeal; they put off preparing their speeches until the last moment, and that's a recipe guaranteeing disaster. So begin by putting your nervous energy into preparing a speech that will please your audience and give you peace of mind. One of the best places to start is by examining the kind of examples that you should aim to avoid.

First of all there's the speaker who only has one speech, which he or she wrote several years ago and to which they have clung ever since. This kind of speech often leaves the audience feeling bewildered and a bit confused about what the speaker actually has to say to *them* — because of course, even with a few changes and adaptations, a speech originally designed to be delivered at a union dinner will not be suitable for a retirement presentation. The jokes, the language, the tone and the style will be wrong, and the audience will sense it. What every audience deserves is a new speech specially designed for the occasion, not some hand-me-down, hacked about in an attempt to make it fit.

The second bad example to avoid is the speaker who 'writes' his speech five minutes before he delivers it. There are some people who can do this successfully, but regrettably few. Those who *think* they can are the tedious types who drone on for as long as they feel like speaking, skipping from topic to topic and boring the audience. They enjoy themselves, but they don't give any pleasure — and giving pleasure is the most important function of the speaker called on to deliver a comic speech.

Before you can begin to plan how to please everyone, give a few minutes' thought to your audience and the occasion.

The audience

Is your audience the kind who will appreciate a complicated tale about your life as a coffee importer, or will they respond more warmly to a more general joke about business? Remember, even if you think your material is brilliant, if the audience don't agree then you'll have problems. So one of the first things to bear in mind is the kind of material they'll enjoy.

Consider their age. The local over-sixties will enjoy nostalgic humour, with lots of references to their younger days, while a group of young whizz-kids will prefer something sharper and more informative. The sex of the audience will affect their response, too. Jokes about secretaries and office scandals will find favour with an all-male gathering, but probably won't go down so well in mixed company. Bear all this in mind when you come to select jokes and material. It may sound obvious, but many a good speech has been ruined by the choice of an inappropriate joke.

As a general rule, avoid all dirty or questionable material that could cause offence. Remember that your

12

reputation could be on the line, particularly if you're speaking in front of an audience of colleagues or other professionals.

Find out as much information about the audience as you can. It's worth your while to contact the organizer of the event and find out from him or her if there's anything special or interesting about the occasion. Is there, perhaps, an anniversary coming up, or some unusual cause for celebration? Is the society, or club or organization involved in anything new or exciting? If it is, make reference to the fact in your speech and try to find some topical quotations or stories to build round it. This can be hard work, and that's why so many speakers don't bother to do it, but it pays off in the end, because topical references prove that you care. They show you've done your research and they make an ordinary speech into a special one for the occasion. The audience will love any 'in' jokes or references you can come up with, and your success will be guaranteed.

The occasion

There are different kinds of speech required for different occasions, and you'll find some guidelines about the kinds of speech to make for a number of occasions in the last part of this section of the book. But 'formulas' alone won't keep you out of trouble. There are a number of other factors that you should bear in mind before you put pen to paper, and they include the tone of the occasion and the mood that you should try to promote. An after-dinner speech, delivered at the end of a pleasant evening of dining and drinking, usually benefits from being fairly robust in tone, whereas a lunchtime engagement might be better served by a sharper, wittier kind of material — particularly if everyone has to go back to work afterwards.

Should you aim for a pushy, aggressive tone, which might go down well at a gathering of fellow professionals and competitors, or would a gentle approach be better received? What kind of mood will the audience be in and what will please them in that mood? These are the kind of questions you must ask yourself when you're weighing up a situation. Just a few minutes' thought could save you from making an error of judgement.

If you have been asked to speak and fulfil some kind of function, like proposing a toast or presenting an award, make sure that you're prepared to do so. This may sound like obvious advice, but some speakers actually forget to do what they're supposed to. They write their speech, intending to tag the toast or the presentation on at the end, but when the time comes they're so overwhelmed by their reception that they leave out the vital bit. Some speakers have been known to sit down still clutching the trophy that they've come along specially to present! The way to avoid this pitfall is to integrate the presentation or the toast in your speech. Instead of just tacking it on, make it the focus of everything you say. Once you've planned your speech in this way make sure that you stick to it. Even if you get a brilliant reception, it's not worth extending or improvising your original plan because it's *that* which will throw you off your stride.

Here's a checklist of 10 simple Do's and Don't's which you should bear in mind as you sit down to prepare your speech:

Do's

1   Do aim to entertain your audience with material and ideas that they want to hear.
2   Do your research before you write your speech, paying particular attention to the age and sex of your audience.
3   What is your role in the proceedings? Have you been invited to propose a toast or give an after-dinner speech?

4   Do give consideration to the tone of the occasion.
5   Do find out about any special guests or facts rele-
     vent to the occasion, and refer to them.

Don't's

1   Don't try to revamp an old speech or use old
     material.
2   Don't include irrelevant or obscure material that
     will bore or confuse the audience.
3   Don't risk offending anyone with dirty or dubious
     material.
4   Don't forget to fulfil the function that you have
     been invited to perform; avoid this by integrating
     the toast, presentation or vote of thanks in your
     speech.
5   Don't plan to improvise any part of your speech or
     be tempted to extend it.

Perfect Preparation

Once you know the kind of speech you're going to make and the sort of audience you'll be entertaining, you can begin to prepare your material. Preparation is absolutely vital if you're going to give a polished performance, so allow as much time as possible to work on the speech.

Start by reading through this book and jotting down all the jokes, quotes, anecdotes and so on that you like and that you feel are directly relevant to your audience. Be ruthless and cut out anything that isn't related in some way to your subject and anything that can't be adapted to fit. On a separate sheet, put down all the things that you *have* to say in the speech and all the points that you particularly want to make.

With any luck you'll begin to see the material falling into place, with the quotes leading into the points you want to make and the stories illustrating the theme. This is exactly what you're aiming for — a seamless speech with one idea moving into the next without any effort. You'll probably have to adapt some of the material if it's to fit in perfectly, so change the names and locations and details to suit the occasion. For example, if you're going to be speaking in Newcastle and you're using a joke set in London, change the location and add some Geordie colour. Most importantly of all, put everything into your own words. You'll feel more comfortable when you come to use the material if it's written in the kind of language and the style you're used to, and it will make your speech seem that much more personal to the audience

Sir Thomas Beecham once said of his orchestra that the important thing was 'to begin and end together, what happens in between doesn't matter very much'. Pretty much the same can be said of making a speech. If you can capture the attention of the audience with your first line, you're likely to have them with you for the rest of the speech. And if they're going to remember anything when they get home it's likely to be your final line — so make sure that it's worth remembering.

Some speakers like to work on the opening and closing lines of their speech together, linking them so that the last line finishes what the first line started. Whatever you decide to do, make sure that both the beginning and the end of your speech are absolutely relevant — both to the occasion and the central part of the speech. Nothing irrelevant should be allowed in at all or you'll begin to look as if you're rambling.

Opening and closing a speech are the two most difficult things of all. Try using one of these opening gambits.

Quotations

You'll find dozens of useful quotations in this book and one of them should be ideal for opening your speech. When you're looking for it, bear in mind that it should allow you to move straight into the main part of your speech without any stress. If you have to force a quotation to fit your theme then forget it. Always inform your audience that it *is* a quote and not your own words. It's quite likely that someone in the audience will have heard it before and they might think you a fraud if you don't name the person who said it first.

Questions

A question can be a very effective way of getting your speech off the ground. Try asking an apparently serious one and following it up with a ridiculous answer. Or ask a ridiculous question to which there's no answer. Whichever kind you choose, aim to raise a laugh from the audience and break the ice.

The 'Did you know?' gambit is also a useful one. Find an amazing fact in the relevant section of this book and ask your audience if they knew it. It's bound to start your speech off with a bang!

Jokes

A joke may seem the obvious way of starting a speech, but in fact jokes can go badly wrong. If they work you'll have the audience eating out of your hand — but if they fall flat you'll have everyone in an agony of embarrassment and praying that you finish quickly.

The best kind of joke to look out for is one that has something to do with a member of the audience or with something directly relevant to the occasion. You may find that simply by changing a few details in one of the jokes in this book you've got the ideal opening gag — in which case use it. But never use a joke simply because you think it's funny.

Exactly the same advice can be applied to ending a speech. No speech, no matter how well-received, can be counted a great success unless it ends on a high note. Looking for a new screenplay, Sam Goldwyn once remarked, 'What we want is a story that begins with an earthquake and builds up to a climax.' That's what you have to aim for too!

Never end with an apologetic, 'Well, folks, that's about it,' line. That only suggests that you've run out of ideas or that you couldn't be bothered to finish the job off properly, and there's really no excuse for that. Even if you can't find the kind of climax that Goldwyn was looking for, you can end your speech in an amusing and tidy way.

Quotations

Don't use a quotation for the opening *and* closing of your speech because that would look too much like cheating, but a quote can round off a speech perfectly. Again, you'll find something suitable in the relevant section of this book — and again, make sure that it ties in completely with the main subject of your speech.

Anecdotes

There's bound to be an anecdote in this book that will encapsulate and illustrate your theme perfectly. You can use it to finish your speech in classic style, but beware of using anything too long or rambling. You don't want to lose your audience's attention in the last few moments. If you're speaking about friends, family or colleagues at work, try to uncover an amusing story about them; nothing embarrassing, of course, just something to show what nice people they are. This is *guaranteed* to bring your speech to a successful conclusion.

Jokes

Ending a speech with a joke is even more risky than opening with one. After all, even if your opening joke falls flat you have the rest of your speech to regain the audience's interest. If you end with a damp squib, however, no matter how good the speech the audience will remember you for only one thing — your failure to pull it off. Only finish with a joke if you can think of nothing better and if you're absolutely certain that it will work.

When you're preparing your speech, take an occasional look at this checklist of 10 Do's and Don't's just to keep your aims in mind.

Do's

1   Do check your material to ensure that it's suitable for the audience you assessed in the last section.
2   Do make sure that you have included all the things you *have* to say — your vote of thanks or the toast, for example.
3   Do adapt all the material to ensure that it's relevant.
4   Do aim to start and finish your speech on a high note.
5   Do credit any quotations you use.

Don't's

1   Don't use any material that isn't relevant to the occasion or will cause offence.
2   Don't start your speech with a joke unless you feel confident that it will work.
3   Don't tail off at the end of the speech; finish properly.
4   Don't use too many quotes or anecdotes from the lives of other people.
5   Don't speak too long; make sure that your speech is the right length.

If, when you finish preparing your speech, you feel confident that you've observed these guidelines, you can be sure that you're halfway towards success. Now all you need to know is how to deliver the speech you've written!

Successful Delivery

Preparing your speech is one thing — and the most important of all — but delivering it is something else. The best speech can be ruined by poor delivery and the thoroughly mediocre made to pass muster by good technique. Fortunately just a few simple measures will ensure that your delivery does your speech justice.

Rehearsal

You don't need to learn your material like an actor, but rehearsal will help you to become familiar with it and iron out any problems that weren't apparent on paper. For example, you may find that a particular sequence of words turn out to be difficult to say, or you might have problems pronouncing certain words — in which case rewrite them.

Try to learn half a dozen key phrases which will take you smoothly from one part of your speech to the next so that you don't keep having to refer to your notes; no matter how nervous you're feeling, this will make your speech seem smooth and practised.

While you're rehearsing, experiment by using your voice to emphasize different points of the speech. Try changing your tone and volume, too, for effect. If you have a tape recorder then use it to tape the various versions of your speech — then you can play them back and decide which sounds the most interesting and lively.

Don't, by the way, worry about your accent. Lots of speakers try to iron out their natural accent, but they forget that the way they speak is all part of their personality. Without it they seem very dull.

As you listen to yourself speaking you'll begin to recognize the most successful ways of delivering certain parts of your speech. For example, the best way of telling your jokes is to do it casually, without labouring them too much. If you feel that there's a rather dull patch in the speech try animating it by changing your tone or emphasis, or even just speeding it up a bit. It's this kind of preparation that will give you polish on the day.

Body Language

No matter how nervous you feel about speaking in front of an audience, you should try not to let them know — and it's the body which most often gives the secret away.

Begin by standing easily with your weight on both feet so that you feel balanced. This way you'll look steady, even if you don't feel it. Your main problem will be what to do with your hands. If you have notes, hold them in front of you at about waist level with one hand. With your free hand, lightly grasp the note-holding wrist. If you're lucky, there will be a lectern of some sort at which you can stand. Rest your hands on either side of it and you'll look very much at ease. Only royalty can get away with holding their hands behind their backs, and you'll look sloppy if you put your hands in your pockets, so don't adopt either of these postures.

If you've no notes and no lectern, just stand with your left hand lightly holding your right wrist in front of you. It looks surprisingly natural and relaxed. Next time you switch on the TV you'll notice how many presenters and comedians use the position!

Notes

The very worst thing you can do is *read* your speech. Comic speeches need a touch of spontaneity, even if they've been prepared weeks in advance and you've been rehearsing for days. Reading a speech kills it dead. It makes the material seem dull, even if it isn't; it prevents eye contact, which is very important in breaking down the barrier between speaker and audience; and it destroys that important sense of a shared occasion, with speaker and audience responding to each other. On top of all that, the very fact that you are reading will indicate a lack of confidence — and your audience will be alerted to your discomfort and share in it.

That said, it's equally inadvisable to stand up and speak without the aid of any notes at all. Nerves can affect the memories of even professional speakers, so don't take any risks. Many people like to write their notes on postcards, using a single main heading and a couple of key phrases to prompt them. If you decide to do this, make sure that you number the cards clearly. You are bound to drop them if you don't, and reassembling them in the wrong order could create all kinds of chaos! Make sure, too, that you write your headings in large capital letters. When you're standing up and holding the cards at waist level you need to take in all the information at a single glance

If cards seem too fiddly, write the main headings of your speech on a single sheet of paper, again using a few key words underneath to jog your memory. You'll know, from your rehearsals, those things you find difficult to remember and those which come easily. Jot down the points you get stuck on. If you're going to use quotations then write them clearly on postcards and read them when the time comes. This ensures that you get them absolutely right and, far from doubting your competence, your audience will be impressed by your thoroughness.

Don't try to hide your notes. Simply use them as

inconspicuously as possible. They prove that you have prepared a speech specially for the occasion and that you care about getting it right — and there's no need to be concerned about that.

On the day

On the day of your speech there are a number of simple precautions you can take to ensure that everything goes smoothly. Some of them may seem quite painfully obvious, but it's the most obvious things that are overlooked, particularly when you're nervous.

Electronic assistance — in the form of microphones and public address systems — needs handling with care. When you accept an invitation to speak, enquire if a microphone is to be provided. If it is, test it before the other guests arrive so that you don't have the embarrassing experience of opening your speech only to find that the equipment isn't working. Make a point of checking how to raise and lower the microphone so that if the previous speaker is a giant or a midget you will be able to readjust it without fuss, and try it out, so that you know how far away from it you need to stand. Microphones have a life of their own. You will have to speak directly into some, while others pick up sounds from several feet away. Find out what sort yours is before you begin your speech.

If the microphone squeals at you, or despite your preparations, booms too loudly or not at all, get it adjusted during your preliminary remarks and wait, if necessary, until the fault has been corrected. It may seem amusing to begin with, but both you and the audience will soon tire of it and you won't have a chance to communicate your humour and personality if no one can hear what you have to say or if everyone is in danger of being deafened.

If you know that you tend to put your hands in your pockets while you're speaking, remove all your loose change and keys so that you're not tempted to jangle them. And make sure that you have a clean handkerchief somewhere about you. A scrap of well-used tissue isn't going to impress the audience when you need to blow your nose.

If you've worked hard to make the opening words of your speech interesting and funny, it would be a great shame to waste them by starting to speak while the audience is still talking and settling down in their seats. So wait for silence, even if it seems to take an age, and when you've obtained it start confidently and loudly so that everyone can hear what you have to say. Whatever you do, don't be hurried. Public speakers talk quite slowly and allow plenty of pauses so that the audience can respond. Take it at a leisurely pace, making sure that you're heard throughout the room, and you'll win the audience's attention immediately.

Some people, but only a very few, are at their best after a few drinks. Unless you know for certain that alcohol will improve your performance, it's probably best not to drink before you speak. Drinking tends to dull reactions and instil a false sense of confidence — and you need to be completely in control of yourself and your material if you're going to make a success of the occasion. Naturally, once you've made your speech and it's been greeted with applause and laughter, you can reward yourself!

Whether you've been drinking or not, accidents do happen. Cope with them by acknowledging them and turning them to your advantage. For example, the speaker who knocked a glass of water over himself brought the house down with the throwaway line, 'Whoops! For a moment there I thought my trousers were on fire!' If someone in the audience drops a glass or falls off their chair, acknowledge it and pause for laughter rather than ploughing on as if nothing has happened.

Although you have prepared your speech in advance, you should be aware of things happening around you and flexible enough to add a topical observation or funny remark if necessary. And the better-rehearsed and more at ease you are with your material, the more confident you'll be about including the odd spontaneous line.

If you follow these guidelines you really can't go far wrong. But here, as a last-minute reminder, is a checklist of Do's and Don't's that will ensure that your delivery will do justice to all the work you've put into your speech.

Do's

1 Do rehearse your material.
2 Do work on your posture so that you look relaxed and comfortable.
3 Do prepare your notes and quotations carefully.
4 Do take simple precautions — like dressing correctly, checking microphones and checking your appearance.
5 Do anticipate any accidents and interruptions and be prepared for them.

Don't's

1 Don't read your speech.
2 Don't make any last-minute attempts to change your accent or your appearance.
3 Don't arrive late or unprepared.
4 Don't start your speech before everyone is ready.
5 Don't drink before you make your speech.

The Right Speech for the Right Occasion

Different sorts of occasion require different sorts of speech. If you don't know how long you should talk for, or the correct form for making a presentation, you will find the following guidelines useful. For informal functions or those not covered in this section, it's best to check with the organizer and find out what he or she is expecting from you. Then aim to give them what they want!

After-dinner speeches

After-dinner speeches are the most difficult for the speaker, but they're also the most rewarding. They allow you to show off your wit and personality with none of the constraints that are imposed by the need to make a toast or present a prize. They're a challenge, certainly, but if you prepare properly they needn't be an ordeal.

When you stand up on your own after a good dinner, with the audience expecting ten or fifteen minutes of pure entertainment, you *must* be prepared. It's quite impossible to be amusing, relaxed and interesting for that length of time unless you've put in hours of work beforehand. What's more, planning and rehearsal will enable you to appear confident, no matter how nervous you feel inside, and appearances are important. A tense, nervous speaker makes the audience feel tense and nervous too. If you look as if you're enjoying yourself you're halfway to convincing the audience that they are too.

Some very experienced speakers are famed for composing their speeches on the back of a menu a few moments before they are introduced to the audience. This is a recipe for disaster unless you're a total extrovert or a professional performer, so it's not a good idea to follow their example.

Another point to remember is that it's not advisable to use your invitation to speak as a platform for your own views. You may well hold strong opinions on important subjects, but you should only expand on them in debate and not in an after-dinner speech, where your job is to entertain, not to pontificate. Keep your material witty and light and try to pace it so that any longer stories are followed by quick laughs. Don't allow yourself to get bogged down.

Try also to be brief. When you are first invited to speak, find out from the organizers how long they expect you to talk for and don't exceed their guidelines. It's better to be brief and very funny than to speak for half an hour with only a few laughs. Make allowances, when you plan and rehearse your speech, for laughter, which will add to the length of time it takes to get through the material. With luck and a sharp pencil you should end up with a speech in which every line counts and there's not a single piece of waffle. Don't worry if it looks *too* brief, either. No one ever complained of a speech being too short!

Sometimes things do go wrong, no matter how much work you put into preparation. A well-known speaker who is normally guaranteed a good reception found himself faced by a silent, inattentive audience when he entertained after dinner at an international company's annual conference last year. Nothing he did seemed to amuse them — but how was he to know that the company's new austerity plan had just been launched and many of those around him were in imminent danger of losing their jobs?

If this kind of thing happens to you, all you can do is cut your losses and sit down. Don't just stop in mid-stream, however. Try to condense your argument or your material, or cut it. Deliver your finishing lines and sit down with your chin up. There's really no point in going on, because it will just make you and the audience even more unhappy.

Presentations

There's a simple formula for presentations, and it can be adapted to suit all kinds of occasions, from retirements to award ceremonies. The main things to include are details of the name and achievement of the recipient, and, if the award is being made on behalf of a company, its origins and donor. Remember that there may be people present who know nothing whatsoever about the background of the person or the event, so be as informative as possible. And don't try to steal the limelight from the person being honoured.

Here is the basic presentation formula being used for an award ceremony.

1   *Name the award, giving full details about its history and sponsors, if there are any.*
    Ladies and gentlemen, thank you all for coming here this evening to witness the presentation of the Kwick, Grabbit and Runn Golden Arrow award for the best young businessman or woman of 1987. As you may know, this stunning trophy, which is sponsored by the local company of Kwick, Grabbit and Runn, is awarded each year to the most promising business-man or woman under the age of 35 in Smogchester. All the entrants have to undergo a gruelling examin-ation of their business knowledge and acumen, as

well as having their current vetures scrutinized by our distinguished panel of judges. (Name them, if necessary.) Last year's winner, I'm pleased to be able to tell you, has already gone on to great things — helped, no doubt, by the *cachet* of his title and the prize of £1,000 which accompanies it.

2   *State the name of the recipient and what he or she has done to merit the award.*
This year's worthy winner is Ivan Orange — and I doubt whether that news will surprise anyone who knows him. Ivan's career as founder and chairman of Orange Enterprises has been quite meteoric. (Give further details, perhaps with a suitable anecdote.)

3   *Present the award.*
I'm very pleased, Ivan, to be able to present you with this beautiful trophy and the title of Kwick, Grabbit and Runn's Young Businessman of the Year — and, of course, this cheque for £1,000.

If you ever find yourself in the pleasant position of receiving such an award, this is the pattern which your answer should follow.

1   *Thank the person making the award and the organization he or she represents.*
I should like to express my thanks to you, Mr Grabbit, to the other members of your company, to the panel of judges and to everyone concerned with the award.

2   *Say what it means to you and what you intend to do with it. Give a few hints about your future plans.*
I'm very honoured and proud to have been chosen to receive the Golden Arrow, which is one of the most highly regarded awards made in the business world. I shall keep the trophy on my desk at Orange Enter-

prises, where I hope it will inspire me to emulate the success of previous winners. Expansion plans for Orange Enterprises are already underway, and I hope to be opening a new factory in Smogchester in the next few months, providing more jobs and wealth for this great city.

Votes of thanks

When it comes to making a vote of thanks after a guest speaker has made his or her speech, you have to break one of the main rules discussed in the earliest part of this book, and that's preparation. A vote of thanks needs to be a spontaneous response to what has just been said, and by definition it can't be prepared in advance.

You can, if you're really worried, do some homework and find out what the speaker is going to talk about so that you're at least prepared for that, but it's best just to listen carefully to what he or she has to say, jot down the things you particularly want to comment on and add any amusing lines or quotations you can think of. To these you add your thanks.

Your main concern should be to prove to the speaker that you have listened to and enjoyed his speech, and to that end it's usually necessary to refer to some of the points he has made, but on no account should you turn it into an action replay of what has just been said. Some speakers, when making a vote of thanks, tend to anato-mize the speech bit by bit, but this is neither necessary nor correct.

If by any chance the speech should have been a flop, keep your thanks as brief as courtesy allows and as appreciative as honesty permits. Don't go over the top with your praise. The speaker and the audience will both be aware of the problem and neither will enjoy salt being rubbed into the wound.

A vote of thanks speech should take five minutes at

the most; any longer and you'll be rivalling the guest's contribution to the evening.

Toasts

A light-hearted toast is required for a great number of informal occasions, including retirement and promotion celebrations and most business- and office-orientated functions. If you're asked to propose such a toast, try to keep it brief — two minutes is about the right length. For this reason, long jokes and stories are not in order, but brief jokes and amusing quotations *are*. You'll find plenty of them in the final section of this book.

As with all other speeches, ensure that everything you have to say is entirely relevant and amusing and leads up to your main function — which is encouraging others to join you in a toast of good health or happiness.

These guidelines should ensure that you make the right kind of speech for most formal occasions. If you're invited to speak at a function and you're unsure what kind of speech is appropriate, always make a point of asking the organizers what they are expecting of you. If you know that, and you aim to please them, you really can't go wrong.

Here is a final checklist of Do's and Don't's to be considered when you're invited to make your speech.

Do's

1   Do start by assessing the audience and the occasion.
2   Do you know how long you're expected to speak for, and on what subject?
3   Are you expected to propose a toast or fulfil a function of some kind?

4 Do your homework.
5 Do it now!

Don't's

1 Don't leave anything to the last minute or rely on making an impromptu speech.
2 Don't forget to find out vital things like people's names and titles.
3 Don't forget to rehearse your material once you've prepared it.
4 Practise looking relaxed and learn to use your notes effectively.
5 Don't forget to include your thanks and acknow-ledgements to everyone concerned.

PART TWO
The Material

Jokes, Jokes, Jokes

In this section you'll find jokes suitable for all branches of business and banking, from bank managers down to bank robbers, and from company chairmen down to shopkeepers. When you find a joke you like, don't just copy it down from the page. Rewrite it in your own words and style, putting in new details of your own and generally ensuring that you make the joke your own — and not just something you found in a book.

The bank cashier had been asked to supervise a new clerk. 'I want you to count this bundle of notes and tell me if there are a hundred,' she said.

The clerk started counting, very slowly, and got as far as sixty-two before handing the rest of the bundle back to the cashier. 'Look,' he said, 'it's all right so far, so it's probably all right all the way.'

A newly-wed couple went to see the bank manager about buying a house. 'I'm earning eighty pounds a week,' said the husband. 'How do we stand for a mortgage?'

'You don't stand,' growled the bank manager. 'You go down on your hands and knees.'

The manager of a large London bank called in one of his young employees. 'Robinson,' he said, 'it has been drawn to my attention that although you earn only four hundred pounds each month you drive a sports car, you wear better suits than some of the senior management, you eat in that smart restaurant over the road each lunchtime and you take exotic holidays three times a year. I know for a fact that your family aren't wealthy. Frankly, I'm worried — and suspicious.'

'There's no need to be, sir,' smiled the young man. 'I'll tell how I do it. There are nearly three hundred people who work here. Each month I raffle my salary and most of the staff pay five pounds for a ticket. By the way, would you like one?'

A young man walked into a High Street bank and asked the manager for a loan. 'Sorry,' explained the manager, 'but you don't have an account with us, and we only make loans to customers with accounts.'

'That's a pity,' said the young man. 'I only wanted to borrow five pounds for three months and I'm willing to leave my car as security. Won't you change your mind?'

The bank manager was intrigued, so he accompanied the man outside. Sure enough there was a brand new car complete with its documents, which were in order. 'All right,' said the manager. 'We'll take the car as security against the loan.'

The stranger left and the car was driven to the back of the bank and parked in the garage there. It stayed there for three months, when the young man returned as promised. He paid the few pence interest on his loan and the bank manager returned the car keys. 'Look, you've puzzled me,' said the banker. 'You could have borrowed five hundred pounds or even more . . .'

'I didn't need it,' said his customer. 'You just tell me where else I could get my car garaged for three months for 50p?'

Mr Jones ran a newsagents shop next door to a bank. One day a customer came in and asked if he could have a loan of ten pounds until the end of the month. 'Honestly, I'd like to,' said Mr Jones, 'but I have this arrangement with the bank. I don't lend money and *they* don't sell news-papers.'

The manager of a country bank purchased a racehorse. In order that he could slip away to watch it running he named it 'Financial Investment'. That way, if anyone needed to see him, his secretary could honestly explain that he was away studying a financial investment.

After a while, though, his secretary received a change of instructions. 'From now on,' said the bank manager, 'if anyone calls for me on race days, tell them I'm out observing an economic crisis.'

Did you hear about the Irish bank cashier who only kept his job for a day or two? The problem was that he used to count the notes, 'One, two, three, four, five, and another one, and another one . . .'

A bank manager's wife accompanied him to a party held by a local businessman. She was distinctly nettled when she saw her spouse smiling at an extremely attractive and rather flashily dressed woman and asked her husband who she was. 'Just someone I met recently in a pro-fessional capacity,' he said.

'Whose profession — hers or yours?'

The bank manager was called out of his office by his secretary to observe where a customer had stumbled into a window and cut himself. 'There's blood everywhere,' she told him.

'Where's he bleeding from?' asked the manager.

'I think he lives locally,' she replied.

A young bank employee was seen leaving a Soho brothel by one of his senior colleagues. The older man warned him that he wouldn't get far in the bank if his habits came to the knowledge of the manager.

'That's all right,' said the young man. 'I was just adding to my banking experience.' The other man looked dubious. 'I *am*,' he insisted. 'I took some professional advice on a short-term association, made a deposit, which was to our mutual satisfaction, settled my outstanding account liabilities and left with an option to renew at some further date. And if *that's* not improving my banking experience I don't know what is.'

The chairman of a large company always asked his ageing assistant to write his speeches for him. The assistant hated the job, and it was unfortunate that the chairman was the kind of man who liked appearing in public, so he had to work hard. In spite of this, and the fact that the speeches were generally very good, the chairman never offered a word of thanks for them and never gave the slightest acknowledgement to his script writer.

One week before the assistant was due to retire the chairman requested another speech for a meeting of computer experts. The speech appeared as usual on his desk and he took it along with him on the night. Everything went smoothly for the first five minutes. The serious points, the references to the success of his own company and topical observations on the economic climate were interspersed with amusing quotes and jokes that had the audience laughing appreciatively. Then the chairman turned the page — only to find, printed on it in capitals: FROM NOW ON YOU'RE ON YOUR OWN, YOU OLD BASTARD.

The extremely elderly chairman of a northern company had travelled down to London for a meeting. Wishing to obtain a breath of fresh air he went for a walk and soon got hopelessly lost. Taking the wrong turn, he wandered into Soho, where he was accosted by a prostitute.

'How old are you, then?' asked the woman.

'I'm just turned eighty,' said the old chap.

'Oh well, you've had it then,' commented the woman, turning away.

'Have I really? How much do I owe you?' said the man.

A business study group was addressed by a successful man who afterwards asked for questions from the audience. He was asked to name some of the people who had influenced him on his way up the ladder of success. Pausing for a moment he then said brightly, 'Well, there was a chap called Johnny Walker, another called Arthur Bell and two fellows called Whyte and MacKay — all good Teachers!'

'There's one thing you should know about me,' said the businessmen. 'I don't like Yes men.'

The new executive nodded understandingly. The businessman held out his hand. 'I like people who say no when I want them to say no!'

A wealthy businessman happened to bump into a poor relation in the street and gave him a ten pound note. 'Thanks,' said the relative, 'but I should tell you that I met your son yesterday and he gave me *twenty* pounds.'

'That's because he has a rich father,' said the businessman.

A young executive who was extremely ambitious and anxious to get to the top of his company, arrived home unexpectedly one afternoon and saw, through the half-open bedroom door, his managing director making love to his wife.

Stunned, he went back to the office, where he soon blurted out what had happened to one of his colleagues. His friend was very understanding. 'It must have been awful for you to have walked in and found your wife being unfaithful with old Brown,' he said.

'But you don't understand!' cried the executive. 'He nearly saw me!'

At the end of a busy board meeting the chairman raised his hand for silence. 'I should like to know who of you here has slept with my secretary.'

There was an embarrassed silence. 'All right,' he said. 'I'll put it another way. Is there anyone here who *hasn't* slept with my secretary?'

One man, new to the board, raised his hand. 'Fine,' said the chairman. '*You* fire her!'

The newly appointed chairman of a group of companies was somewhat nervously glancing at his notes for a speech when he was approached by the toastmaster. Much to his dismay the latter asked, 'Are you ready to speak, sir? Or shall we allow them to enjoy themselves a little longer?'

The company chairman was a pompous chap who always preferred a round of golf to actually sitting down and getting some work done. His poor put-upon assistant had to do everything for him, including writing his speeches. One morning the chairman breezed into the office. 'I'm speaking at a publishers' meeting tonight,' he said. 'I'll need a twenty-minute speech, lots of jokes, with plenty of references to the Booker prize.'

The assistant spent the rest of the day writing the speech and placed it on his boss's desk when he finally went home. The following day the chairman stormed in. 'That was the most appalling speech you've ever prepared for me,' he shouted. 'It was so boring that it had the audience asleep, and what was more it lasted for an hour.'

'Ah,' said the assistant. 'I wonder if that would have anything to do with the fact that I gave you two carbon copies?'

A businessman who'd come up through the East End to found his empire decided to take on as his assistant a public-school educated man. He looked good, he sounded marvellous — but he didn't quite understand the commercial world, as the businessman discovered when, on his first day, the new employee drifted into the office at eleven o'clock.

'You should have been here at nine,' barked the businessman.

'Should I?' asked the assistant. 'Why, what happened?'

Though he'd just left school, the managing director's son was already being groomed to take over the family firm — so it was a terrible shock when he was killed in a car crash. The company's executives immediately went into huddles, scheming about who should take the son's place, but one young man decided to take the bull by the horns. He phoned the grieving father and, after expressing his condolences, suggested, 'I would like, in my own humble way, to be able to take the place of your son — only if it would please you, of course.'

'It would indeed,' said the managing director. 'But before you take his place you'll need to get the undertaker's permission.'

A board of directors were asked to vote on the choice of their new chairman. There were two principal candidates and they both indulged in some unpleasant efforts to persuade their colleagues to vote in their favour. One board member was approached by one of the would-be chairmen and offered an increase of a thousand pounds in his salary if he voted for him. Then the other candidate came along and offered him a five hundred pound pay rise. The board member voted for the second man on the grounds that of the two he was the least corrupt.

People's names can cause all kinds of problems. Take the case of a businessman called Cholmondeley, which is pronounced 'Chumley'. A man called Sidebottom arrived at his office to see him and asked his secretary if Mr

Cholmondeley was in — pronouncing it exactly as written.

'I'll see if Mr "Chumley" is in,' said the secretary, carefully emphasizing the correct pronunciation. 'May I have your name?'

'Yes,' he replied. 'I'm George Sidebum.'

'Hmmm, a salary increase, eh?' said the businessman. 'I expect you've often wondered what you'd do if you had my kind of income, haven't you?'

'No,' said the assistant. 'But I have frequently wondered what you would do if you had mine.'

An old Jewish businessman lay dying. His family gathered round him.

'Mama?' he called.

'I'm here,' she said.

'Manny?'

'I'm here, Jacob.'

'Rebecca?' he whispered.

'Here, Papa.'

'Reuben?'

'I'm here too, papa.'

'Well who the hell,' spluttered the old man, 'is minding the office?'

The personnel manager of a company found himself in an embarrassing situation. A month ago he had agreed to employ a new worker, but by the time the man actually turned up for his first day at the office the company had been reorganized and the position he was intended to fill had disappeared.

'Oh, don't worry,' said the new employee, quite unruffled. 'The little bit of work I do wouldn't be noticed by anyone.'

A pompous old businessman had just taken on a new secretary after his old one had retired — and he was being very fussy about her work. 'Look here,' he ordered when he noted that she had corrected his spelling, 'You're not paid to *think*. Just type down everything and don't change a thing. That's all I ask.'

That afternoon he opened a file of letters waiting for his signature. The top one read:

Dear Mr Zwink — *what kind of a stupid name is that?* — With reference to your letter of — *damn it, what was the date of his last letter? I can't find it. Fill it in later, would you?* — We will certainly be able to fulfil the contract within the specified time at a cost — *Where's the estimate? Oh, maybe I didn't get one. Get Frank on the phone and ask for a quote, then fill it in here. And if this Zwink chap says yes, we'll have to insist on fifty percent up front. He looks a bit dodgy to me.* Thank you for your enquiry. We await the pleasure of your valued order ...

Did you hear about the London businessman with cash flow problems?

'I'm in Queer Street, old man,' he told a colleague.

'Don't worry,' said the friend. 'Why don't you apply for a GLC minority support grant?'

A respected Japanese client was invited to attend the formal dinner held at a London hotel by a major British manufacturer. Unfortunately the Japanese businessman turned up in an ordinary suit, while all the other guests were in black ties.

'I'm so sorry,' said the Japanese, bowing low to the chairman. 'I will go and change. I had not realized you would be wearing your nightdress.'

The businessman had employed a very young and attractive secretary. One day the girl didn't turn up for work — but her mother did.

'Can I help you?' he asked in surprise.

'I'm Belinda's mother,' she announced. 'You're a wicked man! Do you realize that she's pregnant?'

'Oh, goodness,' said the businessman. 'If it's true and she's really pregnant, I'll give her fifty thousand pounds and set up a trust fund for the baby — if that's all right with you?'

'That sounds wonderful,' said the mother. 'And if it should turn out to be a false alarm, will you give her another chance?'

A businessman decided to make his fortune by promoting people with unusual talents. His first signing was a man whose talent was for eating eggs — he could manage four dozen in twenty minutes. The businessman booked a London restaurant and called the press and TV to watch this amazing feat, which would win his client a place in the Guiness Book of Records.

Things started well. The man managed to eat a dozen eggs in just two minutes. The second dozen took a lot longer. By the time he started on his thirtieth egg he was looking quite ill, and as the hands of the clock passed the twenty-minute mark he'd managed to swallow only three dozen. The audience began to pack up and leave, all of them disappointed. 'Sorry, boss,' he said to the irate businessman. 'I don't know what went wrong.'

'But you've eaten four dozen before!'

'I know.' The man shook his head. 'I did it all right at rehearsal this morning.'

The businessman's long-suffering wife got bored with all his boasting when he was made vice-president of his company. 'That's nothing,' she told him. 'Down at the supermarket they have vice-presidents for everything. They even have a vice-president in charge of the pasta.'

Furious, and anxious to prove her wrong, the husband rang up the supermarket and asked to speak to the vice-president in charge of pasta.

'Which one?' came the reply. 'Vice-president of spaghetti, vice-president of macaroni, vice-president of pasta spirals, vice-president of tagliatelle . . .'

The young businessman had got his financial arrangements in something of a mess. In a thoughtless moment he'd loaned a thousand pounds in cash to a friend and hadn't asked for a receipt. Now his accountant and the tax man were pestering him for evidence of the loan, but the friend didn't want to put it in writing.

'What do I do?' the young man asked a colleague.

'Write and say you need the two thousand pounds you lent him,' suggested the man.

'You mean one thousand pounds, that's what I loaned him.'

'No,' said the colleague. 'If you say that he owes you two thousand he'll write back to point out that it's only one thousand — and you'll have the evidence.'

An Irish businessman went to see his doctor about his sexual problem.

'You've been working too hard,' the doctor advised. 'Get some exercise. Try riding a bike a few miles every day.'

Some days later the doctor received a telephone call from the man. 'Has your sex life improved?' he asked.

'How would I know, I'm eighty miles from home by now!'

The businessman had hit hard times and he and his family were just scraping along. As a consequence there were big economies at home.

For Sunday lunch one day his wife dished up two lamb chops with potatoes and gravy. Looking at his two children, the businessman said, 'I'll give you ten pence each if you'll just have potatoes and gravy.' The children jumped at the chance to make some money, so the businessman and his wife enjoyed a chop each.

When the plates had been cleared the wife brought in a delicious steamed pudding. 'Now,' said the businessman, 'Who's going to have ten pence worth of pudding?'

A businessman on a trip to Japan was taken for a drive on Sunday by his host. The scenery was very pleasant, but at one spot they passed a small lake where dozens of very elderly men were swimming and sunbathing naked.

'Good grief!' laughed the businessman, making his host stop the car. 'We wouldn't allow this in England — not in full view of the road, anyway. Isn't it considered improper for people to swim in the nude in public?'

The Japanese businessman tried to be tactful. 'No,' he said, 'but it *is* considered improper for anyone to watch.'

A salesman was trying to convince a small businessman of the necessity of purchasing a machine that packaged parcels automatically. 'It's a false economy not to have one,' he insisted. 'It'll pay for itself in no time.'

'I'm sure,' said the businessman. 'But you see, we're paying for the duplicator with the money we're saving by not going to the copy shop. And we're paying for the computer with the money we save by not having filing and stationery costs. I'm sorry, but at the moment we simply can't afford to save any more.'

A Jewish businessman was playing golf with a customer with whom he was anxious to clinch a deal. He insisted on discussing the matter whilst his opponent was addressing the ball.

'I'll not do it for less than five thousand pounds,' he said as the customer drove his ball, causing him to slice it in the direction of a group of other players.

'Fore,' he shouted.

'All right,' the businessman answered. 'To you four thousand — but there's no need to shout.'

A thrusting young executive had invited his managing director to dinner in the hope of furthering his career. Days had been spent planning the menu and getting the house just right, but the effect was ruined by their small son who appeared on the stairs just as the visitor arrived.

'I wanted to see you,' he said, 'because Mum said you were a self-made man.'

'So I am,' smiled the boss, 'and proud of it.'

'Then why did you make yourself look like *that*?'

A young man who was just about to embark on a business career went to see his grandfather, who had founded the family firm. 'Remember, my boy, that in business honesty is still the best policy.'

'Right, grandfather,' said the grandson.

'But before you do anything else, read up on company law,' recommended the old man. 'You'd be surprised at the kind of things you can do in the name of business and still be honest.'

Two business partners decided to spend one Sunday together fishing. As they sat on the bank waiting for a nibble one suddenly turned to the other.

'I think I forgot to close the office safe!' he exclaimed.

'That doesn't matter,' said the other. 'After all, we're both here.'

The company director was giving some advice to his son. 'There are two things you must remember if you're going to succeed in business, my boy,' he said. 'The first is honesty and the second is sagacity.'

'What do you mean by honesty?' asked the son.

'I mean that you should always keep your word once you've given it, no matter what the consequences.' The boy nodded.

'And sagacity, father?'

'*Never* give your word.'

A young executive was lunching with his boss, who had embarked on a long explanation of how he had succeeded in business.

'When I arrived in this town, young man, I had a brown paper parcel which represented my entire worldly possessions. Within two years I had built three factories, employed two hundred and fifty people, lived in a large detached house and drove a Rolls-Royce.'

'Gosh, that's some achievement, sir,' said the executive. 'Tell me, what did you have in your parcel?'

The boss smiled and puffed on his cigar. 'Two and a half million in cash.'

The small businessman was very worried when two big shops opened on each side of his premises and began to poach his customers. Then one day he had a bright idea. 'All I need to do is change the name above my own shop,' he told his friend. 'I'm having the sign put up tomorrow.'

'What good is that going to do you?' asked his friend. 'Changing the name won't help.'

'But it will,' said the businessman. 'I'm going to call it Main Entrance.'

Two business colleagues were arguing over lunch about the relative stupidity of their secretaries, and finally they agreed to stage a contest to find out which of the two was the most thick.

Back at their offices, the first man called in his secretary, gave her a five pound note and told her to go and buy a word processor with it. 'And make sure you bring back the change,' he called after her.

The second man called in *his* secretary and said, 'Go along to the chairman's office and see if I'm there, would you?' Off she went.

The two secretaries bumped into each other in the corridor. 'Where are you going?' asked one.

'I've got to buy a word processor, though where I'm going to find one at ten minutes to five and the shops about to shut beats me,' said the other. 'How about you?'

'My boss has asked me to go and check whether he's in the chairman's office — though why he can't phone and find out for himself, I don't know.'

A Scottish businessman was giving a Hogmanay party for his employees. As he lived in a flat in a tall block he gave them instructions on using the lift. 'You'll be able to reach the button for my floor with your elbow,' he said.

Puzzled about this, one of them asked why they should use their elbows to push a lift button.

'You'll not be coming empty-handed, I trust,' was the boss's reply.

Two executives were busy discussing whether sex was a pleasure or hard work.

'It's the best thing in life,' said one, a bachelor.

'You wait until you're married,' said the second. 'After a while it just becomes a chore, like everything else.'

At that moment one of the young trainees walked in, so they decided to ask him his opinion. 'Tell us,' they said, 'is sex work or pleasure?'

The young man thought for a moment. 'It's got to be a pleasure, because if it was work you'd be making me do it for you.'

A lawyer who acted as legal adviser to a businessman he didn't get on at all well with, received a call from the man's wife to tell him that her husband had just died. 'The funeral is on Thursday. Are you coming?' she asked.

'No,' said the legal adviser. 'I believe you.'

One London businessman was very fond of a bottle of wine — or two — at his favourite bar at the end of a day's work. One night the barman opened up and two pink elephants, a blue camel and a green and yellow striped rhino walked in.

He looked at his watch and said, 'I'm sorry, you lot, but you're early, he isn't here yet.'

The stockbroker got home from work to find his wife in bed with another man. She looked up and smiled broadly.

'Congratulate me, darling. I've gone public.'

The stockbroker died and went to heaven. On arriving at the Pearly Gates he was greeted by St Peter. 'Before you're allowed into heaven, you have to prove to us that you're eligible for admission,' said St Peter.

'Well,' replied the stockbroker, 'I've done a few good things in my life. I gave a tramp sixpence in 1955. Once when I was drunk I put a tenner in a charity box somewhere. And only the other week I gave an old lady a few bob.'

'Is that all on record?' asked St Peter. His assistant angel checked in the book and confirmed that it was. 'And was this all the good you've done?' he asked.

'I think so,' said the stockbroker.

'In that case,' said St Peter to the assistant, 'just give him his money back and tell him to go to hell.'

A city gent on his way to the Stock Exchange was stopped in the street by a threadbare tramp begging for the price of a cup of tea.

'Look,' he said, giving him a five pound note, 'why don't you get some clean clothing and improve your appearance a bit?'

'Thanks for the advice,' the tramp said, 'but I don't try telling you *your* business, do I?'

The life insurance salesman thought that his son was marrying into a rather dodgy family, but quite how dodgy he didn't realize until the wedding when he announced that he was going to give his boy a free life insurance policy.

'Oh no!' shrieked the bride. 'Don't do it! I don't want Daddy to set him on fire like the warehouse!'

A stockbroker had to take to his bed with a high temperature, which was bad enough to make him delirious. His wife checked the thermometer and raised her eyebrows.

'What is it?' he asked.

'101,' she replied.

'Well, when it reaches 102 sell,' he told her.

The managing director of a small manufacturing company ruled all parts of his organization with a rod of iron. At the end of a particularly stormy management meeting he looked round the boardroom table and said, 'Right, let's vote on the recommmendations. All those in opposition raise their hands and say "I resign".'

The office junior was well-known for his laziness and his lack of punctuality, so when he rolled in at work twenty minutes late his boss was waiting for him.

'What was it this time?' he asked.

'A power failure,' said the junior. 'I got stranded on an escalator for nearly half an hour.'

The company down the road were swindled by their firm of accountants last year, so now they've come up with a new system for doing the books.

A team of specialists brought in from Czechoslovakia will share the job with a high wire act on temporary loan from the circus. The chairman says that he's sure that this system of Czechs and balancers will prevent any further attempts at fraud.

A number of London call girls got themselves organized and formed a company last year, and they've done so well that this year they want to use advertising to enhance their image.

The advertising agency which won the account was puzzled — how could they advertise such services without offending anyone? They decided that for illustrations they'd use tasteful reproductions of classical nudes, but what for a slogan? Then someone had a bright idea. 'Give us the tools and we will finish the job.'

The owner of one of the world's largest biscuit factories

was so proud of his achievement that he would personally escort parties of school children around the plant, pointing out the latest equipment and talking about the booming biscuit market.

He also took great pride in telling the children how he started the business from his back room and built it up to this level. So he wasn't happy to hear a teacher say, as the schoolkids were climbing back into the bus, 'Well, now you've seen it. If you don't work hard and get your exams, you'll end up working here.'

An Irish company decided to invest a lot of money in a new Japanese computer. They were so proud of it that they booked a famous film star to come and set the system in motion. The big day came, and the offices were decorated with bunting, with all the local bigwigs assembled expectantly. The star arrived and after a number of photos had been taken she pressed the button on the main terminal. Nothing happened. Technicians ran around trying to put the fault right. Someone else went off in search of the manual. Finally someone noticed a little tiny notice in the packing case which said, 'Batteries not included'.

Two prostitutes were waiting in the magistrates' court for their hearings. 'How's business?' one asked the other.

'Booming. If I had another pair of legs I'd open a branch in Piccadilly.'

An insurance salesman was, rather unusually, being pestered by a client for a policy. Unfortunately the client concerned was ninety-two and not in a good state of health.

'I'm sorry, sir,' he apologized, 'but we really couldn't take you on. You're too much of a risk.'

'A risk!' protested the old man. 'You just check the stastics and you'll see that very few men die over the age of ninety-two.'

Some years ago an insurance man was approached by a client who wished to take out a policy on himself. He filled in the form supplied but left one space blank — that referring to the cause of his father's death. Puzzled, the insurance man asked him to complete it, but the man was very unwilling.

After a great deal of discussion the insurance broker managed to elicit the fact that the client's father had been hanged. However, the man still refused to have the fact recorded on the form.

'Let's put it this way,' suggested the insurance man. And in the blank space he wrote, 'Fell from scaffold; death instantaneous.'

The tax inspector was checking the income tax return of a single man and noted that he was claiming allowances for a dependent child.

'Is this an error?' he scribbled in the margin.

'You're telling me?' was the reply from the taxpayer.

A farmer met his local vet in the pub and suddenly remembered that he hadn't paid the last bill for innoculating his cows. 'Why haven't I had a reminder from you?' he asked as he wrote his cheque.

'Oh,' said the vet, 'I never ask a gentleman for money.'

'What do you do if he doesn't pay?' asked the farmer.

'After about three months I conclude that I made a mistake and he's not a gentleman — so then I ask him.'

The insurance broker had just tied up a big deal with a carpet manufacturer, agreeing to insure his warehouses for a large sum. As he signed the forms, the carpet dealer said jokingly, 'And what do I get if the place burns down tonight?'

'At least ten years,' said the insurance man.

Two men were up for interview for the position of company accountant. The managing director asked them the same simple question. 'What is ten times ten?'

'One hundred,' said the first man.

'That depends rather on the figure *you* had in mind, sir,' said the second.

The second man got the job.

Arthur worked as a maintenance engineer with a manufacturing firm in Bolton. He came home with a beaming smile on his face and said, 'I've had a grand day at work, love. All sorts went wrong!'

For a long time the departmental manager had been trying to talk Watkins, one of his most reliable employees, into joining the company's private pension scheme.

'It won't cost you a penny,' he explained for the umpteenth time. 'And if you have to retire early you'll get a good income. Just sign — there's nothing to lose.'

'No,' said Watkins stubbornly.

'Do you object for reasons of principle?' asked his exasperated boss.

'No,' said Watkins — and would add no more.

Eventually, hearing of this, the company chairman called Watkins in. 'It's quite simple,' he said. 'Everyone in the company except you has signed, Watkins. It's extremely inconvenient for us to have one exception. If you don't sign, you're fired.'

Watkins obediently signed, and as he left the office his departmental head was waiting for him. 'Did you sign?' he asked.

'Yes,' said Watkins.

'My God, what did he do to make you sign?' asked the boss.

'Let's just say that he put the proposition to me in a new way.'

The personnel manager was interviewing a very smart young public school man. 'What can you do?' he asked.

'I play golf, drink champagne, eat out a lot, go to Ascot

and Henley, make boring speeches, have affairs with my secretary, drive a Porsche . . .'

'Ah, well,' sighed the personnel manager, 'I'm not sure you're right for the accountancy vacancy. But you can start on Monday as managing director.'

It was the first day of Mr Brown's retirement, and already he was beginning to find it a strain. 'No, we can't go to the cinema,' he told his wife when she suggested they go out. 'We don't have the money. We're going to have to scrape to get by as it is . . .'

'Don't worry,' said Mrs Brown. 'I've got a surprise for you. Over the past few years I've managed to save six thousand pounds, and we can enjoy spending it now.'

'How did you manage that?' her husband asked.

'Every time we've made love, I've put some money away in the building society. Over the years it's mounted up. We're going to be quite comfortable.'

Mr Brown clapped his hand to his forehead. 'Why didn't you tell me? If I'd known, I'd have given you all my business.'

The inventor had just come up with an idea for a new children's game and he took it along to an interested company. They sat around playing it for a little while until one of them said, 'I don't know about this. It seems too complicated for children. I can't really understand how it works.'

The inventor was shocked. 'It's a very educational game,' he told them. 'It will prepare children for life in the adult world. You see, whatever they do, it's always wrong.'

A young man was being interviewed for a job. 'It sounds fine,' he told the personnel manager, 'though I must admit that at my last place I was paid more — and the conditions were better.'

'They gave you an hour for lunch?' asked the personnel man.

'Yes.'

'Free life insurance and private health scheme?'

'Yes — and a ten per cent bonus each Christmas, six weeks' paid holiday a year, free travel, *and* we finished work at 2 p.m. each Friday.'

'It sounds perfect!' exclaimed the personnel manager. 'Why on earth did you leave?'

'They went bust.'

The ultra-modern premises of a large company were officially opened by a government minister. It was widely known that the minister's taste in buildings was very conservative, but he said nothing about all the chrome and glass as he was introduced to the chairman, the chief executive and all the senior members of the company. Finally he was introduced to a little man at the end of the line.

'This, Minister, is the chairman of the steering committee responsible for the design of the building.'

The minister shook hands and then, with a meaningful glance at the surroundings, said, 'Yes, steering — but no brakes, I can see that.'

Money Matters

Every bank manager and businessman knows that real life is far funnier than any joke, but if you don't have a real-life anecdote of your own to tell try one of these. They're all true and they're all guaranteed to amuse your audience.

The 1970s were a particularly difficult time for people in British industry and a lot of ventures went under, costing the banks that had backed them large sums of money. One notable exception was the merchant bank Lazards, which had not made the mistake of backing such risky businesses. Asked how he'd managed to make such successful decisions, the bank's chairman replied, 'Quite simple. I only lent money to people who had been to Eton.'

A French dramatist called Tristan Bernard hit hard times towards the end of his life and was obliged to withdraw all his savings from his account at the Banque de France. As he emerged from the bank with every penny he owned in his pocket, he turned to the guard who stood outside. 'Thank you, my friend,' he said. 'You may go home now.'

A Californian bank clerk faced with a bank robber brandishing a water pistol and proffering a hold-up note which read, 'Milk, Bread, Pick up laundry,' politely pointed out that there must be some mistake. The would-be bandit made an embarrassed exit from the bank, but was captured by police as he tried to get his car to start.

The American humorist James Thurber once overdrew his bank account and was summoned by the bank manager, who was stunned to hear that he didn't keep a note of the cheques he wrote.

'Then how do you know how much money is in your account?' he asked.

'I thought that was *your* business,' replied Thurber.

A vigilant French bank clerk helped to catch a murderer when he noticed that some bank notes handed over by a customer smelt funny. They had been stolen during a raid on the home of an eighty-six year old man, during which he had been killed. The old chap had kept his life savings in an old sock — hence the strange smell.

Some years ago in Pennsylvania the local judge was also chief cashier of the local bank. One day a stranger came in to cash a cheque, but his evidence of identity did not satisfy the judge.

'Why, I've known you to sentence men to be hanged on worse evidence than this,' said the man.

'That may be,' replied the judge. 'But when it comes to letting go of cash we have to be mighty careful.'

T.S. Eliot, one of the greatest poets of our century, worked for some time as a junior member of staff at a branch of Lloyd's Bank. He had already had some poetry published and acclaimed when one of the senior bank staff met I.A. Richards, a famous critic, on holiday in Switzerland. They got talking about Eliot, and Richards made it clear that he greatly admired his poetry. The bank official was pleased to hear this and said that he felt that if a man had a hobby it helped him with his work. Eliot was certainly doing well, he told Richards. 'I don't see why — in time, of course, he shouldn't become a branch manager,' was his conclusion.

Groucho Marx hated the clichéd and meaningless phrases that pepper business letters. Once, having received a letter from his bank manager with the standard, 'If I can be of any service to you, please do not hesitate to call on me,' ending, he wrote back:

> Dear Sir,
> The best thing you can do to be of service to me is to steal some money from the account of one of your richer clients and credit it to mine.

During the 1960s Jerry Rubin was the scourge of middle-class America. As the long-haired leader of the Yippies he stormed into the New York Stock Exchange and lectured stockbrokers on his 'revolutionary socialist movement'.
  In 1980 the very same Jerry Rubin started a new career as a securities analyst on Wall Street at a salary of $36,000 a year, and declared, 'Money and financial interest will capture the passion of the 1980s. Let's make capitalism work for everybody.'

A Belgian businessman made a successful career for himself, but he could never forgive his parents for once calling him stupid. To taunt them, he regularly sent them generous cheques on which he carefully made an error — like getting the date wrong or 'forgetting' his signature.

Sir Bernard Docker, the wealthy British industrialist, left Britain in 1967 for life as a tax exile on Jersey, full of the delights of the island and the wonderful time he intended to have there. Two years later he and his wife announced that they were leaving. 'They're the most frightfully boring, dreadful people that have ever been born,' complained Lady Docker of their fellow tax exiles.

Mr Sidney Long of Worthing, Sussex, had a brilliant idea in 1972 and accordingly placed his mail order advertisement in the newspaper.

'Convert your dead, cold, black and white TV into a multi-coloured fantastic picture,' it read — and all for two pounds. Unfortunately one of the people who bought this amazing invention turned out to be a consumer protection inspector — and he didn't agree that a piece of multi-coloured polythene which was intended to be stuck over the TV screen was quite the miracle that Mr Long had promised!

An American millionaire decided to invest some of his money in a little culture, and consequently provided the backing finance for an up-market production of a Eugene O'Neill play. The first time he saw what he'd backed was on the opening night — and it wasn't an O'Neill play that was performed but a frothy French farce.

Going backstage, he made his complaint to the manager, who just shrugged. 'You know how these things get changed around a bit in rehearsal,' he explained.

In 1972 Mark Spitz won seven gold medals at the Munich Olympics for his performance in the pool. The world seemed to be his oyster. Signed up by a Hollywood agent, plans were made for him to endorse products, develop his own brand of sportswear, appear on TV shows and, eventually, become a film star. The best-laid plans can backfire, however, as he and his advisers discovered. Mr Spitz is now a dentist.

In the early years of this century a successful Nottingham cigar manufacturer was approached by a competitor with the suggestion that they go into partnership to produce a new product to be called the cigarette. 'They'll never become popular,' the cigar manufacturer said dismissively — so John Player had to go it alone.

In 1874 an inventor named John Keely came up with an idea for creating 'inter-atomic ether' and 'vibrating energy' which, when properly harnessed, would facilitate technological miracles. Among his planned projects was an engine that would power a ship across the Atlantic fuelled by just a pint of water.

Wall Street speculators grabbed the chance to make money from such scientific marvels and invested a million dollars in Mr Keely — who soon died from too much of the good life. The speculators raided his laboratory in the hope of discovering some of his amazing secrets — only to find all the demonstration equipment phoney. Far from being powered by 'inter-atomic ether', Mr Keely's models were fuelled by compressed air, fed to the equipment from a hidden tank via carefully concealed tubing. His backers had wasted their money.

A story is told of the inventor Edison who took a friend for a ride through a scenic valley.

'It's a beautiful valley,' said the friend.

'Well,' said Edison, 'I'm going to make it more beautiful. I'm going to dot it with factories.'

Henry Ford, founder of the motor manufacturing industry, once set sail for Europe in a Peace Ship accompanied by other famous pacifists. Their intention was to bring World War I to an end by appealing to the various heads of state. Unfortunately the plan didn't work and the ship became known as the Ship of Fools. Ford, however, was unrepentant when he got back to the USA just three weeks after he had left. 'I didn't get much peace,' he said, 'but I learned that Russia is going to be a great market for tractors.'

On a trip to Dublin, Henry Ford was asked if he'd care to contribute to a fund to build a new orphanage. He did so willingly and made out a cheque for two thousand pounds. His generosity made the headlines of the local paper — but the sum he had donated was erroneously quoted as *twenty* thousand pounds.

When the fundraiser came to apologize and offered to put the matter straight, Ford told him not to bother and promptly wrote another cheque for eighteen thousand pounds. 'There's just one condition,' he said before he handed it over. 'When the new building opens, I want this inscription on it: "I WAS A STRANGER, AND YOU TOOK ME IN."'

Andrew Carnegie, the American businessman, believed in the responsible use of wealth and was renowned as a great philanthropist, but his patience was worn thin by a fervent socialist, who once visited him and talked at great length about the evils of capitalism.

Wearily Carnegie sent one of his assistants out to research two lots of figures — one, an estimate of his wealth and the other the latest estimate of world population. Then he made a quick calculation and instructed his secretary, 'Give this gentleman sixteen cents. That's his share of my wealth.'

In 1979 Nelson Bunker Hunt and a syndicate set out to capture the silver bullion market. They bought all they could and stored it in a Texas vault, and within a year the price had increased by nearly eight times.

'I'm not a speculator, I'm a market squeezer. I am just an investor and holder in silver,' Hunt told his critics. Alas, the Washington powers-that-be didn't like his style of business, and changed regulations governing private investment in bullion.

The Hunts lost a billion dollars, the largest personal dealing losses in history, but Nelson didn't seem too bothered. 'A billion,' he told the world, 'is not what it used to be.'

Hetty Green was a nineteenth-century millionairess who made much of her fortune on the stock market. So good was she that people used to ask her advice. To one hopeful who requested her to name a really good investment, she replied, 'The other world.'

Deciding to vary his business a little, Alfred Bloomingdale, owner of the world-famous department store, produced a musical which opened out of town before its planned transfer to Broadway. The critics panned it, and when Bloomingdale asked the advice of George S. Kaufman he was told, 'If I were you, I'd close the show and keep the store open at night.'

When the American Celanese Corporation decided to get into the European paper industry they started by buying a huge forest of eucalyptus trees in Sicily for pulping, and then built a mill on site. It all went smoothly, and soon they had a local workforce waiting to start. Then, and only then, did their expert business team arrive to look the place over. And what *they* saw cost the company many millions of pounds. Because the eucalyptus trees, the reason for the mill and the operation, were only a few inches tall — and for the next twenty years, until they grew to maturity, wood pulp had to be imported from Canada.

Harold Alexander, who was governor of Canada and Minister of Defence, finished each day in the office by tipping the remaining contents of his 'In' tray into his 'Out' tray. Fascinated, his assistant couldn't help asking why.

'It saves time,' explained Alexander. 'You'd be surprised how little of it ever comes back.'

A hapless robber recently tried to obtain money from three small local businesses — but without luck. At the first shop he handed his hold-up note to the girl behind the till, but she refused to take it, believing it to be an obscene suggestion. At the second the Asian shopkeeper apologized but said that he could not read English. At the third the proprietor hunted for his glasses and couldn't find them, so had to turn the robber away. He went home in disgust.

Deciding to expand their business to the European market in the 1940s, Campbells the soup manufacturers shipped several million cans of their condensed soup to the UK. Unfortunately British housewives didn't understand the principle of condensed soup. They took one look at the small cans, which sold for the price of a large can of ordinary soup and rejected Campbells' as over-priced.

Businessmen tend to judge people by their appearances, which can be a mistake — as this story illustrates.

A shabby gentleman turned up at the National Gallery one day with a painting under his arm. He asked to see the governor but was rudely refused, and only after he had waited patiently and repeated his request was he allowed in.

Having reached the governor's office he explained that he wanted to give his picture to the National Gallery and began to unwrap it. However, the governor did not want to see it and told him curtly either to leave it or take it away, as he was too busy to waste time. The old man tried to persuade him to take a quick look there and then, but he firmly refused and was on the verge of having him removed from the office when the covering fell off — revealing a masterpiece that the governor had tried but failed to buy.

'My name is Sir William Wallace,' said the shabby gent quietly. 'I came to offer this picture to the National Gallery.'

Having to leave the room in the middle of a business meeting can be very embarrassing, but Dorothy Parker found a way of coping with it. 'Excuse me, I have to go to the bathroom,' she said, rising to her feet. 'Actually I have to telephone, but I'm too embarrassed to say so.'

The opera star Maria Callas, who was born in the USA, brought up in Greece and sang in Italian and German all over the world, was asked by a reporter what language she thought in. 'I count in English,' she replied.

In 1980 Lindi St Claire, a London prostitute who specialized in 'disciplining' willing gents, registered her enterprise as a company. She wanted it to be registered with a frank description of its nature, but the nearest the prudish registrar would come was 'personal services'. Annoyed, Ms St Claire went to court, where the judge ruled against her.

Sadly her bad luck did not stop there. The Inland Revenue noted the court case, visited her west London premises, which contained a fully-operative dungeon with whips and a rack, and presented her with an income tax bill of £10,000.

Hungarian insurance companies were still wrangling about who was responsible for an unusual accident for some time after it was over. The accident occurred at a railway crossing. A horse and cart, a man in a sports car, a motorcyclist and a farmer with a goat all paused at the lowered gates of a level crossing. The farmer tied his goat to the barrier and was having a quiet cigarette when the train roared through, terrifying the horse, which bit the motorcyclist. The motorcyclist hit the horse, which provoked its owner to jump down and start a fight with him. Meanwhile the horse backed into the sports car, whose furious driver joined the scrum. The farmer stepped in to try to pull them apart and meanwhile the barrier rose, taking the goat with it. Before they could get it down the goat was strangled. Claims for compensation were registered by all parties.

A Lieutenant Colonel in the Swedish airforce invented a device that saved his service millions — and so he was rewarded with a sum of $40,000. However, this didn't turn out to be the generous gift it first appeared.

The tax man immediately took $30,000. The remaining $10,000, when added to his salary, put him in a higher tax bracket, so another $7,000 was knocked off. To add insult to injury, it was then decided that he would have to pay social security and other taxes on it. By the time they'd finished with him, his invention had cost *him* $13,000.

Professor Agassiz, the great Swiss zoologist and geologist, was invited to go to New York to give a lecture. He declined, explaining that he was too busy. The invitation was repeated, and this time a large fee was offered too. Again the professor declined, with the words, 'I simply have no time to earn money.'

Peter Altenberg was an Austrian poet with a strange hang-up. Although he was not a poor man he was an obsessive beggar. One of the people he solicited on each occasion they met was fellow poet Karl Kraus, who always refused him. One day they met and, as usual, Altenberg begged for some money. 'I'd gladly give it to you, but I really, *really* don't have the money,' Kraus said.

'Very well, I'll lend it to you,' said Altenburg.

Borrowing money can affect a relationship. Joseph Addison, the British writer and politician, once lent a friend some money — and before long he began to notice a change in the man's behaviour. Before the money had changed hands they had frequently disagreed on a number of subjects. After the loan the friend agreed with everything Addison said. This annoyed him, and one day when the friend concurred on a subject which Addison knew for certain they had previously disagreed on, he said, 'Either contradict me, sir, or pay me my money.'

The playwright Richard Brinsley Sheridan was always in terrible debt. He was once cornered by a tailor who demanded at least the interest on his bill. 'It is not my interest to pay the principal, nor my principle to pay the interest,' said Sheridan.

Gertrude Lawrence, the actress, once found herself in Woolworth's with a basketful of purchases and no cash. 'Charge it,' she told the assistant, only to be told that there were no charge accounts at Woolworths.

'Then how on earth have you all managed to stay in business so long?' she asked.

Bing Crosby was appearing on a chat show when the interviewer complimented him on his calm and relaxed air. Was there a secret to this? he wanted to know.

Crosby took out a huge wad of banknotes. 'That helps,' he said.

When they heard that the Marx Brothers were to make a film entitled *A Night in Casablanca*, Warner Brothers threatened to sue them on the grounds that it was too similar to their own film, *Casablanca*. Groucho Marx replied, 'I'll sue *you* for using the word Brothers.'

Dorothy Parker, famous for her wit, once had a job that involved working alone in a dingy little office in the Metropolitan Opera House building in New York. No one ever came to visit her, and she became so depressed that when the signwriter came to paint her name on the door she persuaded him to write GENTLEMEN instead.

An American swimwear company thought they'd come up with something new and exciting when they launched the 'trikini' in 1973. Consisting of two stick-on bra cups and a pair of briefs, the trikini was demonstrated to potential buyers at a New York swimming pool. After a lengthy explanation about the unique design which would ensure that the cups stayed in place, the model jumped into the pool — and surfaced wearing a monokini.

In 1977 Billy Carter decided to cash in on his big brother Jimmy's success in the White House by launching 'Billy's Beer'. Unfortunately it hit the market just as President Carter's administration went into a nosedive — and sales weren't helped by the comments of Miss Lillian, their mother, who told the world, 'I tried it once, but it gave me diarrhoea.'

Many years ago, when the Pepsi-Cola Company was in terrible financial trouble, Coca Cola was offered the chance to buy them out. They figured that Pepsi couldn't last long anyway and turned down the takeover opportunity. Now Pepsi and Coke are arch-rivals and share the world market almost equally. Someone, somewhere, must be kicking themselves . . .

Quote Me On That

Who said that the idea of space travel was utter bilge? Find this and other business bloomers in the following section, which is packed with business and banking quotations. Whether you need words of wisdom, and wit, or proof of terrible errors of judgement, they're all here.

Bankers are just like anyone else, except richer.

Ogden Nash

Barclay's Bank Burma House will be closed on Friday 11th June due to the official opening of the premises.

Notice in the Daily Nation, *Kenya*

A bank is a place that will lend you money if you can prove that you don't need it.

Bob Hope

What's robbing a bank compared to founding one?

Bertholt Brecht

Banking may well be a career from which no man really recovers.

J.K. Galbraith

It is rather a pleasant experience to be alone in a bank at night.

Willie Sutton, bank robber

A banker without money is like a doctor without pills.

George Woods

I think any man in business would be foolish to fool around with his secretary. If it's someone else's secretary, fine!

Senator Barry Goldwater

I don't meet competition, I crush it.

Charles Revson, American businessman

Next time a man says that his word is as good as his bond, take his bond.

Lord Hume

He was a self-made man who owed his lack of success to nobody.

Joseph Heller

We have yet to find a significant case where the company did not move in the direction of the chief executive's home.

Ken Patton, reporting on business re-location

Chas H. Bond Ltd
Non-ferocious Metal Merchants

Business letter head

The rich are different from you and me because they have more credit.

John Leonard

The salary of the chief executive of the large corporation is not a market award for achievement. It is frequently in the nature of a warm personal gesture by the individual to himself.

J.K. Galbraith

A businessman needs three umbrellas — one to leave at the office, one to leave at home, and one to leave on the train.

Paul Dickson

Nothing is illegal if 100 businessmen decide to do it.

Andrew Young

Experience teaches you that the man who looks you straight in the eye, particularly if he adds a firm handshake, is hiding something.

Clifton Fadiman

It's a religion as well as a business.
Robert Woodruff, chief executive of the Coca-Cola company, on his product

A verbal contract isn't worth the paper it's written on.

Sam Goldwyn

Promotors are just guys with two pieces of bread looking for a piece of cheese.

Evel Knievel

Statistics indicate that, as a result of overwork, modern executives are dropping like flies on the nation's golf courses.

Ira Wallach

Never invest your money in anything that eats or needs repairing.

Billy Rose

There are two times in a man's life when he should not speculate: when he can't afford it and when he can.

Mark Twain

The City is not a concrete jungle, it is a human zoo.

Desmond Morris

Copper prices picked up yesterday as fears of a quick peace in Vietnam receded.

Daily Telegraph

Anyone who thinks there's safety in numbers hasn't looked at the stock market pages.

Irene Peter

We must believe in luck. For how else can we explain the success of those we don't like?

Jean Cocteau

Business without profit is not business, any more than a pickle is a candy.

Charles F. Abbott

The real leader has no need to lead — he is content to point the way.

Henry Miller

Corporation: an ingenious device for obtaining individual profit without individual responsibility.

Ambrose Bierce

The fact that a business is large, efficient and profitable does not mean that it takes advantage of the public.

Charles Clore

To be a success in business, be daring, be first, be different.

Marchant

A dinner lubricates business.

Lord Stowell

In business, the competition will bite you if you keep running; if you stand still, they will swallow you.

William S. Knudson, chairman of General Motors

Business underlies everything in our national life, including our spiritual life. Witness the fact that in the Lord's Prayer the first petition is for daily bread. No one can worship God and love his neighbour on an empty stomach.

President Woodrow Wilson

Do other men for they would do you. That's the true business precept.

Charles Dickens

Business is other people's money.

Delphine de Girardin

People always live for ever where there is an annuity to be paid to them.

Jane Austen, Sense and Sensibility

If someone asks me, 'What is two and two?', I answer, 'Are you buying or selling?'

Lord Grade

If you can count your money then you're not a really rich man.

Paul Getty

If you would know what the Lord God thinks of money, you have only to look at those to whom he gives it.

Maurice Baring

When I was young I thought money was the most important thing in life: now that I am old I know that it is.

Oscar Wilde

What's worth doing is worth doing for money.

Joseph Douglas

Never in the history of human credit has so much been owed.

Margaret Thatcher

Bing doesn't pay income tax any more. He just asks the government what they need.

Bob Hope on Bing Crosby

A fool and his money are soon headlines.

Anon.

Why does a slight tax increase cost two hundred dollars and a substantial tax cut save you thirty cents?

Peg Bracken

When you make the mistake of adding the date to the right column of the accounts statement, you must add it to the left side too.

Accountants' maxim

It takes twenty years to make an overnight success.

Eddie Cantor

Success is simply a matter of luck. Ask any failure.

Earl Wilson

There are two kinds of statistics, the kind you look up and the kind you make up.

Rex Stout

A gold rush is what happens when a line of chorus girls spot a man with a bank roll.

Mae West

Behind every successful woman there's a man trying to stop her.

Anon.

The Swiss are not a people so much as a neat, clean, quiet solvent business.

William Faulkner

A 10,000-aspirin job.
Japanese way of grading the difficulty of an executive's job

The only place where success comes before work is in the dictionary.

Vidal Sassoon

Economy: cutting down other people's wages.

J.B. Morton

The two most beautiful words in the English language are, 'Cheque Enclosed'.

Dorothy Parker

Work expands so as to fill the time available for its completion.

Parkinson's Law

There is now so large and so involuntary an element of altruism in the making of money, that the process is in some danger of going out of fashion. The more we make, the less of it we are allowed to keep for ourselves.

The Times

A trade union is an island of anarchy in a sea of chaos.
Aneurin Bevan

I've never consciously striven for worldly success. But once I was aware I had it I must say that I'm terrified of losing it.

Gilbert Harding

Beneath every successful man is a woman.

Anon.

I have a lot of respect for that dame Delilah. There's one lady barber that made good.

Mae West in Going to Town

Throughout history people have been making disastrous business decisions. Here are just a few of the worst bloomers.

Space travel is utter bilge.

Sir Richard Woolley, 1956

It is a project which, as far as I can see, has a viable marketing opportunity ahead of it.

Giles Shaw, Northern Ireland's Minister of Commerce, on the De Lorean car

No Civil War picture ever made a nickel.

Irving Thalberg, turning down Gone with the Wind

You'll never get anywhere with a daft name like that.

Arthur Askey to The Beatles

I tell you flatly, Elvis can't last.

Jackie Gleason

Who the hell wants to hear actors talk?

H.M. Warner

There is only one thing about which we can be absolutely certain in the future — and that is the continued supply of cheap petroleum from the Middle East.

Anonymous economist, 1965

You'll Never Believe It!

Some of the things people do in the name of business defy description — and certainly belief! In this collection of strange facts and bizarre stories you'll find at least one related to your own area of business or banking.

In 1981 the Bank of England paid out more than £600,000 to people who had ruined bank notes. One of the worst culprits was the washing-machine, followed by dogs — and lawnmowers.

Security staff at the Fifth Federal Reserve Bank were invited to a conference aimed at finding ways of making bank employees safe from armed robbers. An argument broke out at some point, tempers flared, guns were pulled — and by the time it was over, one man was dead and three seriously injured.

The staff of a Montreal bank celebrated a wedding not so long ago, when clerk Gerry Cash made an honest woman of one of his colleagues. You see, he made Miss Crook into Mrs Cash.

The National Westminster Bank nearly found themselves in hot water with the City planning department when photos of their new building, the tallest tower in London, were submitted to the planners. The fuss was because of a number of statues which had been placed on top of the block. Permission hadn't been granted for *them*, stormed the planners. Then someone took a closer look and noticed that the statues were in fact workmen ...

A Los Angeles bank robber made a serious mistake after obtaining cash from the bank clerk. Instead of grabbing the money and running, he told the clerk to deposit the money in his own account.

A Spanish bank clerk who received sudden promotion to manager, took revenge on his ex-boss by demoting him to the position of office boy. Among his new tasks, the ex-boss had to copy out the local phone book by hand. Fortunately an industrial tribunal forced the new manager to pay compensation.

The tellers at a bank in Nashville, Tennessee, were watching an educational film entitled, 'Tips on How to React to a Holdup'. While they were absorbing the film's message, two masked robbers sneaked in and stole $12,000 from the tills.

In 1959 the head of the International Monetary Fund decided that world inflation was over.

In 1983 a bank robber strolled into a bank in Reno, Nevada and pushed a written note across the counter. The teller read the demand and put the money from his till into a bag, which he handed to the robber, who calmly made his getaway. After such an efficient robbery you can imagine his surprise when he found the police waiting for him when he arrived home. He had written his hold-up note on the back of an envelope — and on the front was his name and address.

Another robbery was foiled by the inefficiency of the Post Office. The would-be robber sent instructions by first class post to the manager of a branch of Barclays. If the manager did not comply with the demands by a predetermined time, the letter read, a bomb planted in the bank would be exploded. In fact the letter didn't arrive on the bank manager's desk until an hour after the supposed bomb was set to explode ...

In 1983 an Irishman, who had an account with the Midland Bank in Newcastle, decided he would rob the branch. He got in all right, but he fell asleep and was found with just £2.64 of the bank's money the next morning.

Also in 1983 an American bank manager received a telephone call saying 'I will explode a remote controlled bomb in your bank unless you deliver $100,000 to the restaurant opposite.' The bank employee who answered the phone was perplexed and explained that there was no restaurant opposite the bank. 'Oh,' said the voice. 'Sorry, I seem to have the wrong number.'

When Henry Ford showed off his first car, crowds gathered, yelling, 'Get a horse!' Thirteen years later he launched the Model T — and the world grated unwillingly into the age of the car.

A Brighton antique dealer, aware that his window display was a temptation to smash and grab thieves, put reinforced glass in the frames. One would-be raider didn't realize this — until the brick he'd thrown at the window bounced back and knocked him cold.

Success in business makes some people very odd. Paul Getty, one of the richest men in the world, had public call boxes installed in Sutton Place, his sumptuous home, so that guests couldn't make free phone calls.

Lim Bim Sung must be one hell of a businessman. He

convinced a number of people in Rangoon, Burma, that he'd bought an old NASA rocket and was running trips to the moon. Someone actually handed over the money for the fare . . .

A Hertfordshire businessman hated the horrible smell that came from the sausage-skin factory at the end of his garden, so he bought it, intending to turn it over to a more acceptable use. Unfortunately he had overlooked a bye-law that limited its use to the boiling of blood, the breeding of maggots, and the preparation of glue and manure.

A British businessman made the mistake of marrying just before Christmas. Unfortunately the pre-Christmas season was so busy that he didn't have time to go on honeymoon — so his new bride went with his mother.

An American businessman used his credit card to place a long distance call from a booth in an airport. Later, when his telephone bill arrived, he was stunned to find that it was for $20,000 and ran to 334 pages in which each call was detailed.

The phone company agreed to investigate and finally came up with an explanation. Two Marines had been in the next telephone booth at the airport, and they'd overheard and made a note of his credit card number. They'd also passed on the details to their friends in the force, all of whom had been using the businessman's account to make their calls.

Business can be a matter of life and death. The Thai representative of the Pepsi Cola Company was shot and killed during a business discussion with his rival, the representative of the Coca Cola company.

A cinema manager once wrote to a newspaper complaining about the phasing-out of the practice of playing the

National Anthem after a film show. He wasn't concerned on grounds of patriotism, however. Apparently when the National Anthem was played people vacated the cinema in a hurry. With no National Anthem, he and his staff had to hang around longer after the film had finished.

The Pentagon once paid $659 for an ashtray. A hammer available for $7 in the shops cost the Washington government $435.

In the 1970s the Hunt Wesson Food company decided to launch their pork and beans product on the French-Canadian market. It was known in America as Big John's, so one of the advertising men suggested that they turn it into Gros Jo's for the new market. Everyone agreed that the new name was catchy and a whole campaign was planned around it. Fortunately, before it was launched a French-speaking employee pointed out that colloquially Gros Jo's meant 'big tits'.

In America the name Betty Crocker is synonymous with home baking. Her name appears on cookery books, recipe cards and a whole range of baking products — yet she does not, and never has existed! Years ago a flour manufacturer invited people to write in for advice on their cooking problems. Thousands did, and a team of staff wrote personal replies to every one. But who, they wondered, should sign them? In the end they devised the name Betty Crocker, which sounded homely and reliable — and one of America's most famous cooks was born!

Who says that British firms are inefficient? A British company once took an order to supply 1,800 tons of sand to Abu Dhabi.

Some spectacular business opportunities have arisen out of unlikely backgrounds. For example, a British aristocrat returning from India brought with him a special recipe for a spicy Indian sauce. At home in Worcester he asked two local chemists to make it up for him and served the resulting mixture to his friends — who thoroughly enjoyed it.

Soon it was so popular that the chemists asked if they might produce it for commercial sale. The aristocrat agreed, and today the sauce can be found in millions of kitchens throughout the world. What was it? The chemists' names were Lee and Perrins, and they named the sauce after the county in which they lived — Worcestershire.

Office space is so expensive in central London that to rent the space taken up by the average waste-paper basket for a year you would have to pay around £50.

Someone has calculated that if a rumour was started at midday in the office and was repeated within two seconds by everyone who heard it to two other people, who repeated it — and so on, by about six-thirty the same day everyone on earth would have heard it. Which is a good reason for avoiding office gossip.

Investigating the disappointing sales of the Cortina, Ford were distressed to discover that translated into Japanese Cortina means 'Broken down old car'. At least they were able to correct their error when it came to the Caliente, a new model designed for launch in Mexico. Just in time someone remembered that in Mexican-Spanish *caliente* is slang for street-walker. Rolls-Royce suffered the same problem with their Silver Mist. In German it means what in polite circles is described as 'human waste'.

The Illinois Committee on Efficiency and Economy was disbanded in 1955 for reasons of efficiency and economy.

A waitress in a Dublin nightclub thought her ship had come in when a wealthy Pakistani businessman gave her a cheque made out for a million dollars as a tip. Before she could cash it, however, the businessman cancelled it.

There is a solicitor in London called Wright, Hassell and Co.

A Church of England vicar impressed his congregation by ripping a five pound note into small pieces to demonstrate the worthlessness of money. What they didn't know was that he gathered up all the pieces and took them along to his local bank to claim the money back.

Insurance firms must have quaked at the news that a Florida man was sueing God for $25,000 after being injured in an accident described by his insurers as an Act of God. A local priest offered to give evidence, but in the end the defendent failed to turn up at the court.

In 1984 British Rail opened a new station costing over a million pounds at Sandwell and Dudley, West Midlands. The Area Manager turned up to officially open the station by boarding the inaugural train. The media attended in force and members of the public waited to climb aboard the first train, which arrived absolutely on schedule. There was just one problem — the driver did not stop at the new station.

A Welsh factory put up a suggestion box in which workers could post any ideas for improving the place. One of the first suggestions was that the suggestion box be removed. It was.

In 1972 a Texan man received a letter from General Motors asking him to take his car back to the supplier as there might be a fault which would make the rear axle fall off. This he duly did, and halfway to the dealer's the rear axle fell off.

The vacuum flask has become an everyday item, but when William Dewar first invented it his mother-in-law, for one, didn't have any faith in it. When he gave her one as a present and told her that it would keep its contents warm for hours, she made a woolly cosy to fit over it.

The Consumer Product Safety Commission in the USA planned a campaign to publicize the danger of badly made and designed children's toys. As part of the campaign they had 80,000 brightly-coloured badges made. Unfortunately someone didn't do the necessary research. The badges were not only printed with lead paint but their pins kept springing open — and they had dangerously sharp edges. The whole lot had to be scrapped.

A businessman who equipped his chain of American grocery shops with electronic tills that *told* customers how much their bills were, discovered too late that he had made a mistake.

The customers didn't want to *hear* what they'd spent — it was bad enough paying anyway, without having it announced to the entire shop.

In 1979, so it was rumoured, Lord Grade spent more on making the doomed film *Raise the Titanic* than the ship itself had originally cost.

Certain publishers must kick themselves whenever they see an episode of M.A.S.H. on television. The book of M.A.S.H., which spawned the film and the TV series, was turned down by no fewer than twenty-one publishers before someone realized its potential. Four publishers turned down Frederick Forsyth's *The Day of the Jackal* before Hutchinson dubiously took it. So far it's sold more than eight million copies.

The Israeli Post Office came unstuck in 1970 when the

issued a stamp with *Yahweh* printed on it. Licking God's name is forbidden — and so is destroying it. The Post Office had to arrange for the useless stamps to be stored in a vault.

Business Briefs

This section is full of brief jokes and one-line remarks for you to slip unobtrusively into your speech. They're ideal for breaking the ice when you first get up in front of your audience and also for linking your various themes and ideas. Use them interspersed with longer jokes to ensure that the laughs keep coming. The best way of telling these jokes is to drop them casually and move on quickly, leaving it to your audience to spot them. They'll appreciate your relaxed style, as well as recognizing your professional technique.

One of my friends has just bought a gift for the manager of the listening bank. It's a hearing aid.

Two Irish bank robbers were so bad at arithmetic they didn't know how much money they had stolen until they saw the newspaper accounts of their raid the following day.

Would you say that the first banking transaction in history was when Pharaoh received a cheque at the bank of the Red Sea which had been crossed by Moses and Company?

'Stand still!' shouted the Irish bank robber as he aimed his gun at the manager. 'This bullet cost me a lot of money.'

Definition of a bank: an institution that will lend you an umbrella when the sun's shining and demand it back as soon as it begins to rain.

Our bank manager is so mean that when he was asked to make a donation to the local orphanage he sent along two orphans.

First Law of Banking
Those who can add up become cashiers.
Those who cannot become inspectors.

Second Law of Banking
Someone *always* pays in three hundred pounds worth of ten pence pieces just after you have sent down for more from the strongroom.

First Law for Bank Customers
Whichever queue you stand in, it's the wrong one.

Second Law for Bank Customers
Whichever queue you stand in, the others all move more quickly.

A new gang of workmen started at the Royal Mint last week. They began the job of starching all the five pound notes. The government has decided that it's the only way of strengthening sterling.

Did you hear about the retired bank manager who bought a bungalow? He called it Duncountin. It was next door to a bungalow owned by a retired hire purchase trader. *His* place was called Mon Repossession.

The secretary of a local cycling club has just gone to prison. He took the bank manager for a ride.

Did you hear about the bank manager who was robbed by

the lady who came in to tidy the offices? She took him to the cleaners.

What's the difference between a fortune-teller and a bank-teller? The first one has his palm crossed with silver and gazes into the future. The other palms your silver and looks 'past it'.

The regional manager had so little confidence in one of the bank's new managers that he ordered that his name should be written on the door in chalk.

Have you heard about the randy computer programmer? He handled hardware, software and underwear.

An inexperienced cashier
Said, when the bank closed, 'Oh dear,
Tis no credit to me,
But my entries I see,
Don't agree with the money in here.'

Always remember that you can make fifty excellent decisions during a working day, but people will only remember the single bad one.

A businessman owes it to himself to become a success. By the time he has made it he probably owes it all to his bank.

My bank manager calls himself the loan arranger and his assistant Tonto.

Did you hear about the shop keeper who decided that his shop front display was too low? He had his facia lifted.

Sign seen on a greengrocer's counter:
GOD HELP THOSE WHO HELP THEMSELVES

I went to a wedding the other week. The businessman accompanied his daughter down the aisle, but before he gave her away he insisted on a receipt from her would-be husband.

Did you hear about the boss who fired five secretaries in a row because of the mistakes they wouldn't make?

The secretary in this office is so beautiful and so willing that she's had an affair with practically every man in the department. In fact she spends more working hours on her back than Michaelangelo.

Did you hear about the Irish businessman who made his fortune with the one-piece jigsaw puzzle?

Would you agree that Noah was the first successful company director? After all, he floated his company while the rest of the world was in liquidation.

If you owe one hundred pounds you're broke.
If you owe one thousand pounds you're in business.
If you owe a million you're a millionaire.
And if you owe a billion you're Chancellor of the Exchequer.

Did you hear about the managing director who tried to kill the company chairman? He was fired, but later they decided to give him a second chance.

You've got to admire my boss. If you don't, you don't work here any more.

The man I work for is the kind that grows on you slowly — like warts.

Our boss is so mean that if he accidentally pays you a compliment he immediately demands a receipt.

Have you heard that Sir Clive Sinclair has just launched a new car driven by electricity? It's small, neat and easy to drive, ideal for business purposes. Unfortunately it has to tow a trailer with a ton of flex on it.

Some of the latest headlines from the business columns:
INTERNATIONAL TRACTORS ENTER NEW FIELD
AVON RUBBER CHEQUES BOUNCED
P & O FLOAT NEW VENTURE
BRITISH AEROSPACE WELL UP
BRITISH RAIL RUNS OUT OF STEAM
SUPERMARKET STOCKS FALL TO DANGEROUS LEVEL
EUROFERRIES CROSS OVER CHANNEL LINK

The question we've all been asking. Will United Biscuits crumble?

W.H. Smith was in the news the other day — and vice versa.

Would you agree that the outlook for Guinness is black?

English China Clay hardened on the Stock Market yesterday, but Marley came unstuck. Boots were on their uppers and Arthur Bell Ltd. dropped a clanger.

My financial adviser is rather old and sometimes gets things muddled up. When I asked what to do with my savings he told me to put them in intrustment vests. And the other day he phoned me up to tell me about progress on the Joe Downes index ...

Did you hear about the speculator who ran into trouble because, though his long-dated stocks were up, his shorts were down?

An engineering firm has just come up with a new business machine. It's called a digital extraction unit and it makes employees pull their fingers out.

Notice seen in the typing pool:
   BECAUSE OF A FLU EPIDEMIC WE ARE SHORT-STAFFED. WOULD MANAGERS PLEASE TAKE MAXIMUM ADVANTAGE OF TYPISTS BETWEEN 10 A.M. AND 3 P.M.

All good business thrives on teamwork. That way there is always someone else to blame when things go wrong.

Beware! Microchips do sometimes go wrong. In fact you can't always count on your calculator.

If all the Scottish businessmen in the world were laid end to end, they still wouldn't reach for their wallets.

My boss is the opposite of yoghurt — at least yoghurt has culture.

At a long meeting it's always wiser to close your eyes and let everyone believe you have been asleep than to open your mouth and prove you *have* been.

The dumb blonde who worked in the City thought that share allotments were where people grew vegetables. She thought a discount market was like Asda. Once her boss asked her to find out the price of copper on the London Market and she spent a whole day trying to find a policeman in Petticoat Lane.

The Board of Directors met to discuss two important proposals for the future of the company. After half an hour they had narrowed the proposals down to eighteen.

Our office manager is a very nervous man. Each morning

when he gets in he has to have a large gin to steady his hands so that he can get the top off his tranquillizers.

The recent cold spell did a lot of unexpected damage. The local pawnbroker received a bill from the council for a cracked paving stone outside his shop. One of the brass balls on his sign fell off.

The Inland Revenue has just bowed to pressure and simplified their tax returns. In the future they'll read: A) How much do you earn? B) Send it.

Life assurance: a way of ensuring that you're poor while you're alive but filthy rich when you die.

Did you hear about the insurance broker who was a black belt at judo, could drink fourteen pints of Guinness straight off, follow them up with six whiskies, then take on six strong men at arm wrestling and wipe the floor with them — what a wonderful woman!

Money may be the root of all evil — but a man needs roots.

Confucius he say man with yen for sex in Sweden must change currency.

Have you heard about the dwarf who spent his time in Soho studying the prostitutes in the area? He describes himself as a micro pro-assessor.

Job advert: YOUTH WANTED TO TRAIN AS PETROL PUMP ATTENDANT. ELDERLY MAN WOULD SUIT.

She's the kind of woman who climbed the ladder of success wrong by wrong.

Is Hambros Bank where pig farmers like to keep their money?

Our secretary is so thick she thinks that tap stock is water and a marketing programme is a shopping list.

Have you heard about the Investment Banker whose wife left him because he didn't generate enough interest?

She was only an insurance agent's daughter, but she was extremely well endowed.

Heard about the man who went to see his bank manager, showed him a white sweet with a hole in the middle, and said he knew how to make a mint with it ...

Our local postman has just been sacked. He kept writing 'Oh yes they do!' on envelopes marked PHOTOGRAPHS DO NOT BEND.

Job advert: FULL TIME OR PART-TIME WOMEN/GIRLS REQUIRED TO WORK IN THE CRUMPET DEPARTMENT.

Never put off till tomorrow what you can avoid altogether.

He who steps on others to reach the top must have excellent balance.

Where there's a will, there's usually Capital Gains Tax.

The best things in life are for a fee.

Did you hear about the girl who earned her living in the iron and steel trade? She couldn't iron very well, but she could steel plenty.

Why is a lift in an office-block like a dance hall? Because no matter how many executives are crammed into it their prime concern will be the ball room.

Always be sincere in business, even if you don't mean it.

Remember, though you can fool some of the people all of the time and all of the people some of the time, you can make a fool of yourself any time.